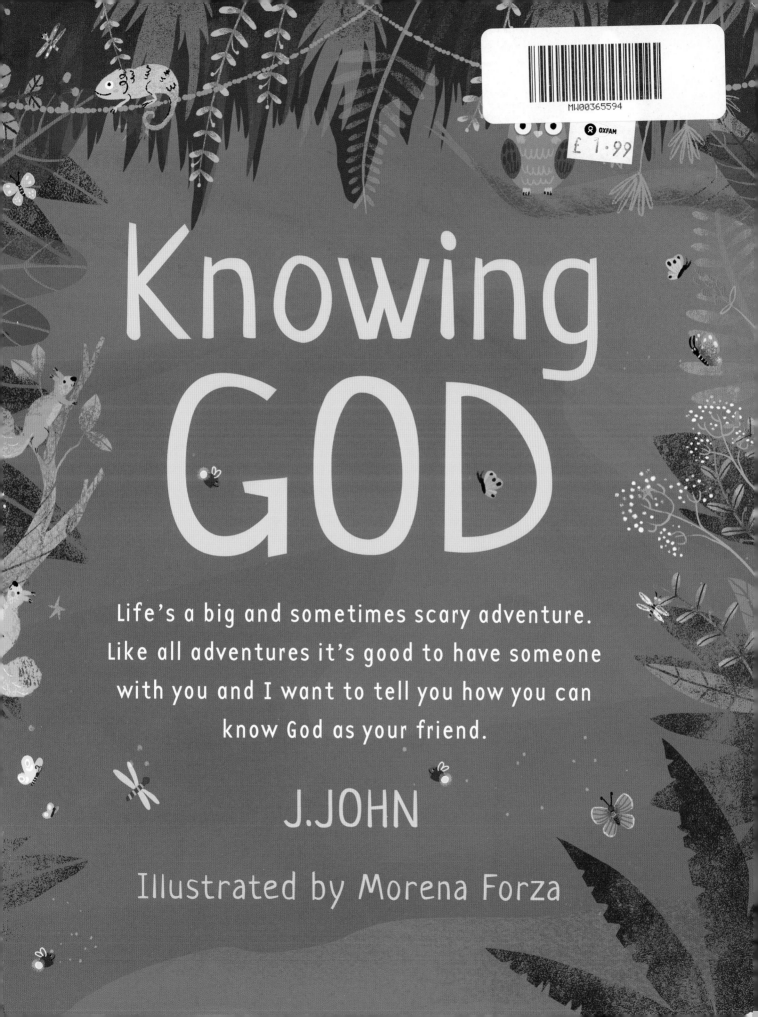

Knowing GOD

Life's a big and sometimes scary adventure.
Like all adventures it's good to have someone
with you and I want to tell you how you can
know God as your friend.

J.JOHN

Illustrated by Morena Forza

About God

Let me begin by telling you some
important things about God.

First, God is BIG. In every way.
After all, he made the universe
and he looks after it.

He runs everything from the enormous bits
– stars, galaxies and solar systems – to the
little things like rain, insects and flowers.
He is also everywhere all the time.
You can talk to him in your mind
and he will hear you.

Second, we can know about God because he has spoken to us.

In the past he spoke through special people and those words are found in the Bible, which is a book that tells us about God, what he has done and how we can know him.

God still speaks through the Bible but sometimes God speaks to us in our minds, sometimes through the words that other people say, and even sometimes through dreams. God also speaks and acts through the Holy Spirit and he became a human being in Jesus Christ.

Third, God is a *person*. He is not a force, a thing or something like a computer program.

He is someone we can know, talk to and be friends with. We can also offend him and make him sad.

Fourth, God is *good*. He doesn't lie, cheat or let you down. He can be trusted.

The last and really big thing to know about God
is that he loves human beings. In particular,
he loves you and wants
to be your friend.

About Us

A long time ago, when God made human beings, he wanted men and women to obey him by loving each other and looking after his beautiful world. God gave rules to guide people in how to live the right way. Sadly, people chose to break the rules and instead of doing what God wanted they did what *they* wanted to do.

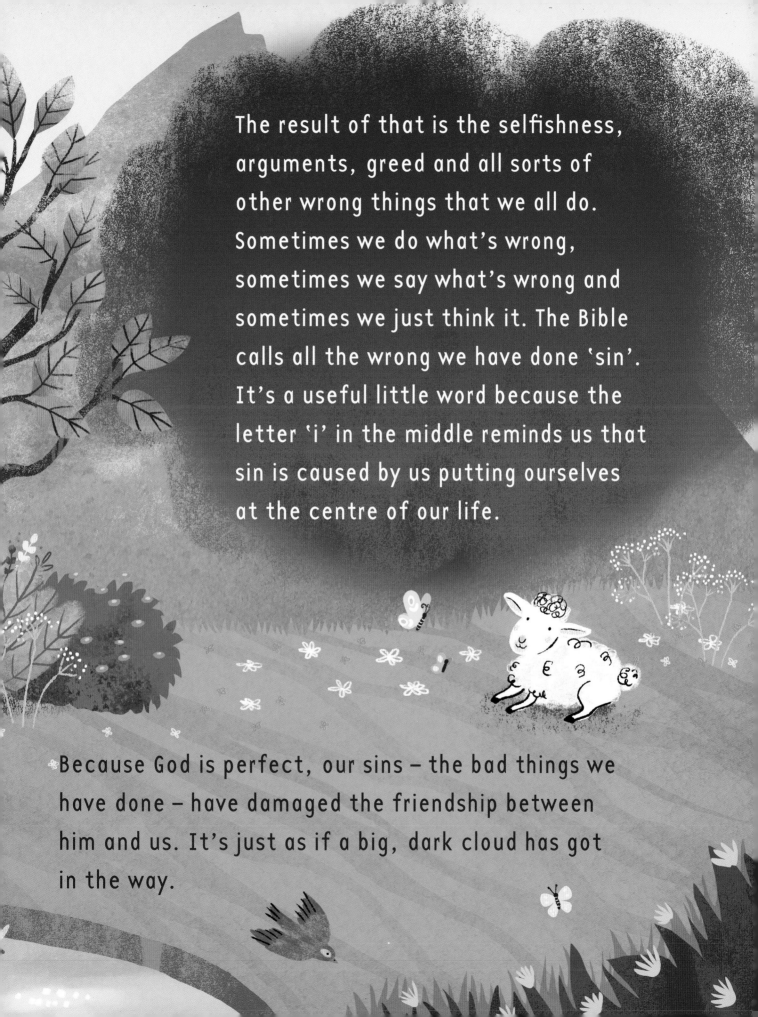

The result of that is the selfishness, arguments, greed and all sorts of other wrong things that we all do. Sometimes we do what's wrong, sometimes we say what's wrong and sometimes we just think it. The Bible calls all the wrong we have done 'sin'. It's a useful little word because the letter 'i' in the middle reminds us that sin is caused by us putting ourselves at the centre of our life.

Because God is perfect, our sins – the bad things we have done – have damaged the friendship between him and us. It's just as if a big, dark cloud has got in the way.

Two thousand years ago, God came to earth as a real person, Jesus Christ, so that everyone could see what a perfect life looked like. The four Gospels – Matthew, Mark, Luke and John – in the New Testament of the Bible tell us how Jesus lived. The Bible teaches that this life is not all that there is. After death there is a second life that goes on forever.

Every one of us will spend that second life either with God or separated from him. To be with God – in heaven – will be amazing because he is good and the only things that are going to be allowed in heaven are good things like joy, peace and love. On the other hand, to be separated from God will be terrible because without God there will be nothing that is good and only things that are bad.

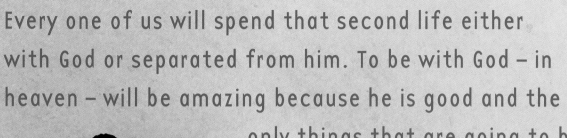

About what God did

When people went against God he could have abandoned them, wiped out everybody and started all over again. But he didn't. God started a rescue plan.

Then, around the date we now call AD 0, Jesus was born in a miraculous way through the work of the Holy Spirit. Jesus taught people about how to live in a way that would please God. He said that he was the only way to God and that he *was* God. He also promised that those people who trusted him would not only know God in this life but be with him forever.

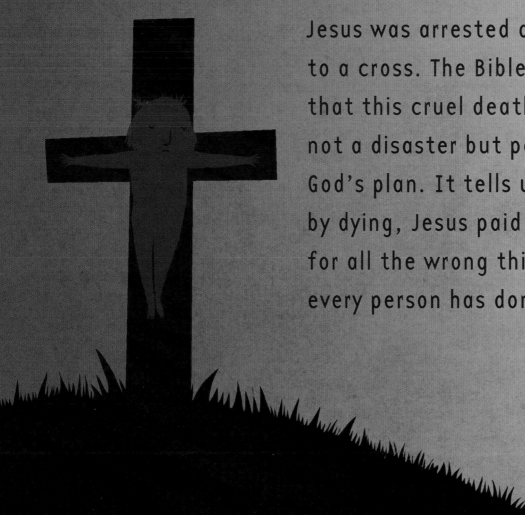

Jesus was arrested and nailed to a cross. The Bible teaches that this cruel death was not a disaster but part of God's plan. It tells us that, by dying, Jesus paid the price for all the wrong things that every person has done.

On the third day after Jesus died, something incredible happened. Jesus came back to life and for forty days appeared to many different people. It was God's way of telling everyone that, despite his horrible death, Jesus was God and someone they could trust. It was proof that Jesus was stronger than even death itself.

Before returning to heaven Jesus told his followers to tell people about him. For two thousand years Jesus' followers – Christians – have been following him and his teaching.

About what we should do

Jesus wants everybody to know him and be his friend. But it's not automatic; you have to ask and accept it yourself. One way of doing this is an ABC.

A Admit that you have done wrong things and you are sorry.

B Believe that Jesus died for you on the cross so that you can be forgiven.

C Commit yourself to following Jesus. It means doing your very best to obey Jesus and being prepared to say that you are one of his followers.

The best way to do this is to pray to God.
Pray this prayer if you want to know God.

Lord Jesus Christ, I realise that you want me to know you and to love you. I admit that I have done, said and thought bad things and that there are many good things that I could have done but I didn't do.

I am sorry and I thank you for dying on the cross to forgive me.

Come into my life now by your Holy Spirit and make me clean, so that I will know your presence, peace and power. Please guide and help me today and every day of my life.

Thank you, Lord Jesus.
Amen.

If you prayed this prayer, WELL DONE. You are now God's friend and you can be proud to call yourself a Christian, which means a follower of Jesus Christ.

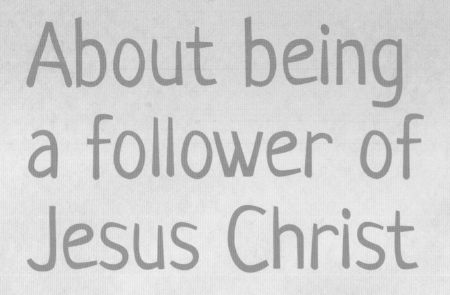

About being a follower of Jesus Christ

Making a commitment to Jesus
is only the beginning. Like running a race,
the main part is not starting the race
but getting to the finish. So let me
give you some guidance.

First of all, don't rely on your feelings. Many people when they make a decision to follow Jesus feel wonderful. Others feel nothing. God wants us to trust him and follow him whether we have good feelings or not. He is a God who keeps his promises.

• *Remember* when you become a follower of Jesus *everything* changes. You are no longer separated from God but you have become a member of God's family. You can now talk to him with confidence because he loves you and listens to you. Always remember God is with you.

- *Read the Bible.* To find out more about God and Jesus and how to live, you need to read the Bible. I recommend you start reading the Gospels and then the letters that follow them.
- *Reach out* to find other Christians. A good way to do this is to join a church.

Finally, let me encourage you.
I made a decision to follow Jesus
forty-two years ago. It has not always
been easy but it is the best decision
I have ever made. Living my life as a friend
of God through Jesus has been an amazing
adventure. And I pray it will be an
amazing adventure for you too.

J.JOHN

Published in 2017 by Theology for Little People, Philo Trust, Witton House, Lower Road, Chorleywood, Rickmansworth, WD3 5LB, United Kingdom

ISBN: 978-0-9933757-8-1

Illustrated by Morena Forza
Design Management by Jeni Child, www.jenichild.com
Print Management by Verité CM Ltd, www.veritecm.com